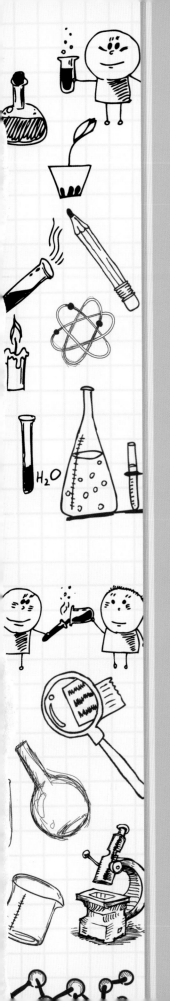

Learning Playground

Fun with Numbers

WORLD
BOOK

a Scott Fetzer company
Chicago

www.worldbookonline.com

World Book, Inc.
233 N. Michigan Avenue
Chicago, IL 60601
U.S.A.

For information about other World Book publications,
visit our website at **http://www.worldbookonline.com**
or call **1-800-WORLDBK (967-5325).**

For information about sales to schools and libraries, call
1-800-975-3250 (United States);
1-800-837-5365 (Canada).

Library of Congress Cataloging-in-Publication Data

Fun with numbers.
    p. cm. -- (Learning playground)
  Includes index.
  Summary: "An activity-based volume that introduces
such mathematical concepts as addition, subtraction,
multiplication, division, fractions, and statistics.
Features include a glossary, an additional resource list,
and an index"--Provided by publisher.
  ISBN 978-0-7166-0228-6
  1. Arithmetic--Juvenile literature. I. World Book, Inc.
QA115.F95 2012
513.2'1--dc22
                    2011004731

STAFF
Executive Committee
President: Donald D. Keller
Vice President and
  Editor in Chief: Paul A. Kobasa
Vice President, Marketing/
  Digital Products: Sean Klunder
Vice President, International: Richard Flower
Director, Human Resources: Bev Ecker

Editorial
Associate Manager, Supplementary
  Publications: Cassie Mayer
Editor: Daniel Kenis
Researcher: Annie Brodsky
Manager, Contracts & Compliance
  (Rights & Permissions): Loranne K. Shields
Indexer: David Pofelski

Graphics and Design
Manager: Tom Evans
Coordinator, Design Development and
  Production: Brenda B. Tropinski
Senior Designer: Isaiah Sheppard
Associate Designer: Matt Carrington
Photographs Editor: Kristine Strom

Pre-Press and Manufacturing
Director: Carma Fazio
Manufacturing Manager: Barbara Podczerwinski
Production/Technology Manager:
  Anne Fritzinger

Learning Playground
Set ISBN: 978-0-7166-0225-5

Printed in Malaysia by TWP Sdn Bhd, Johor Bahru
1st printing July 2011

Acknowledgments:
The publishers gratefully acknowledge the following sources for photography.
All illustrations were prepared by WORLD BOOK unless otherwise noted.

Cover: Dreamstime; Shutterstock

Ton Koene, Alamy Images 18; Ashley Whitworth, Alamy Images 14; Dreamstime 4,
5, 6, 7, 8, 14, 20, 22, 26, 36, 37, 46, 48, 58; Shutterstock 4, 5, 6, 9, 14, 17, 18, 19, 22,
23, 27, 28, 29, 30, 31, 34, 35, 36, 38, 39, 40, 42, 43, 44, 47, 50, 51, 52, 53, 54, 55, 56,
57, 59, 60, 61; SuperStock 21.

Table of Contents

There is a glossary on page 62. Terms defined in the glossary are in type that **looks like this** on their first appearance on any spread (two facing pages).

Numbers Everywhere

You can find numbers all around you. Competitors often wear numbers to identify themselves.

What would we do without numbers? We couldn't even count! We couldn't keep track of birthdays or measure size or amount.

Think of all the numbers you use every day. You read books (like this one!) with numbered pages. Numbers describe the time and the channel of your favorite TV show.

You probably play games that use numbers. You might roll dice or spin a spinner and count how many spaces to move on a game board. In many sports, the team or player with the highest number, or score, is the winner.

Numbers are used in games like dominoes.

There are more numbers than you could count in an hour, a day, or even a lifetime. Think of everyone that lives in your city. They all have different telephone numbers! The street you live on may be many miles long, but no other building on your street has exactly the same address, or number, as the one you live in.

Numbers also tell how much something costs. They tell how much flour to use when you bake a cake. They tell how tall you are, how much you weigh, and how old you'll be on your next birthday! The world is truly full of numbers.

When you call someone, you enter a telephone number that identifies the person you're calling.

People put candles on a birthday cake to represent their age.

Counting

Long ago, people didn't have words or symbols for specific numbers. But over time, people's lives changed. They needed to count sheep, baskets of grain, and other important items.

There are many ways to count numbers. Today we count numbers based on 10's. This counting system is useful because human beings have ten fingers.

The numbers 1 through 10 have special names in most languages because people learned to count by using their fingers. They would count up to 10 fingers and then start over.

In English, the words for the numbers after 10 are based on the first 10 numbers. Eleven comes from an Old English word that means "one left over after 10," 12 means "two left over after 10," and so on.

The number system we use today is based on 10's.

You can use your fingers as digits to count.

Say the numbers 13 through 19. Do you hear the "10" in each one? Thirteen means "three and 10." What does 14 mean? Twenty means "two 10's" and 30 means "three 10's." What do you think 40 means?

One hundred is a special name for ten 10's. One thousand is a special name for ten 100's.

Look below at the chart of some number words in other languages. You can see that 1 through 10 are special numbers, and the other numbers are based on them.

	1	3	6	10	16	30
Spanish	uno	tres	seis	diez	dieciséis	treinta
French	un	trois	six	dix	seize	trente
German	eins	drei	sechs	zehn	sechzehn	dreissig
Arabic	wahid	tsalatsa	sitta	ashara	sittata ashar	tsalatsoun
Japanese	ichi	san	roku	juu	juuroku	sanjuu

Try this!

Imagine you are living thousands of years ago. Nobody has invented the words or symbols for numbers yet. How would you count?

Gather a certain number of objects, such as crayons, marbles, or pasta in a box. Then try to tell a friend how many objects there are—without speaking or writing. Try it with more than 10 objects.

Tools for Counting

Ancient merchants counted such objects as baskets of grain using pebbles or other small objects.

Imagine you are a rich merchant living 3,500 years ago. You have 37 baskets of grain in your warehouse. You just bought 11 more baskets of grain from a farmer. You want to know how many baskets of grain you have now. How can you find out?

First you draw two grooves in the sand with your finger. Then you place seven pebbles in the right groove. Each pebble stands for one basket of grain.

In the left groove you place three pebbles. Each pebble in the left groove stands for 10 baskets of grain.

In ancient times, people in parts of Africa used seashells to count.

The pebbles in the two grooves show that you have three 10's (30) plus seven 1's (7), or a total of 37 baskets of grain in your warehouse. Now you add pebbles for the 11 baskets of grain you just bought. You place one more pebble in the right (1's) groove and one more pebble in the left (10's) groove. Then you count the pebbles in each groove.

There are four pebbles in the 10's groove. Four 10's (10 + 10 + 10 + 10) equal 40. There are eight pebbles in the 1's groove. Eight 1's are 8. So you have 40 + 8, or a total of 48 baskets of grain.

Pebbles and grooves were an early form of a counting tool called an **abacus** (AB uh kuhs). The abacus was invented by people in many parts of the world.

Necklaces of beads made from shells were used by Native Americans to keep records and decorate garments.

The Babylonians, Egyptians, and Chinese used the abacus thousands of years ago.

MAKE YOUR OWN ABACUS

The **abacus** has been used for thousands of years to help people count. Try this activity to make your own counting tool.

MATERIALS

- 4 craft sticks, each about 4.5 inches (11.4 centimeters) long
- 5 bamboo skewers
- 50 pony beads
- Ruler
- Pencil
- Wood glue

DIRECTIONS

1. Starting 1/4 inch (0.6 centimeters) from the end of one craft stick, mark a line with your pencil every inch (2.5 centimeters). You should end up with five lines.

2. Put glue on each of the lines. Glue the ends of each of the bamboo skewers onto the craft stick. Be sure to keep the sticks straight and parallel (the same distance apart everywhere).

3. Glue a second craft stick to the same end of the bamboo skewers so that they are secured between the two sticks. Let the glue dry.

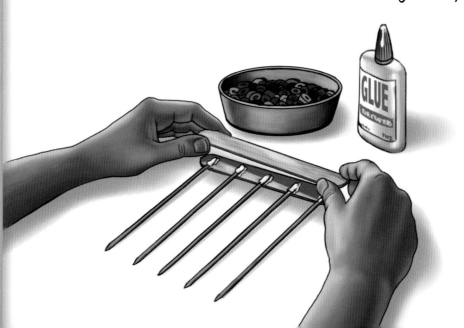

4. Slide 10 beads onto each bamboo skewer.

5. Put glue on the open end of the bamboo skewers. Glue the last two craft sticks to the end just like the ones you've already glued at the other end. Let the glue dry.

You now have an abacus that can count very big numbers! Each bamboo skewer represents a different **place value:** ones, tens, hundreds, thousands, and ten thousands. You can mark each column's place value at the top or bottom of your abacus.

Count by sliding the beads to the opposite end of the stick. Once all 10 beads on a stick have been counted, return them to the other end of the stick and slide one bead across the next stick to indicate an increase in a value of 10. Try adding and subtracting using this method.

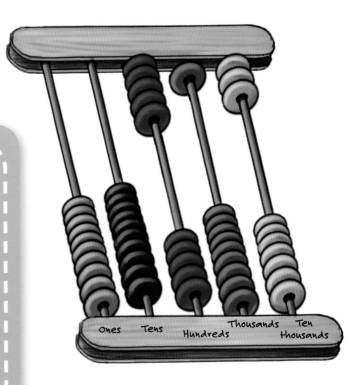

Ones   Tens   Hundreds   Thousands   Ten thousands

What Are Numerals?

Once people began to count, how did they remember the numbers they had counted? They needed a way to write down the numbers—so they invented **numerals.** Numerals are symbols that stand for numbers.

Some of the first numerals were invented by the Egyptians about 5,000 years ago. Their marks for the first nine numbers look like pictures of fingers.

The Egyptians had special symbols for the numbers 10, 100, 1,000, 10,000, and 100,000. A picture of a lotus flower was the numeral for 1,000. There were thousands of lotus flowers in Egypt's Nile River. So the Egyptians probably thought a lotus was a good symbol for a big number like 1,000.

The numeral for 100,000 was a picture of a tadpole. Lots of frogs lived along the Nile River. When their eggs hatched, the water must have been full of tadpoles. That may be why the Egyptians used the tadpole as their symbol for a huge number like 100,000.

The chart on the right shows what the Egyptian numerals looked like.

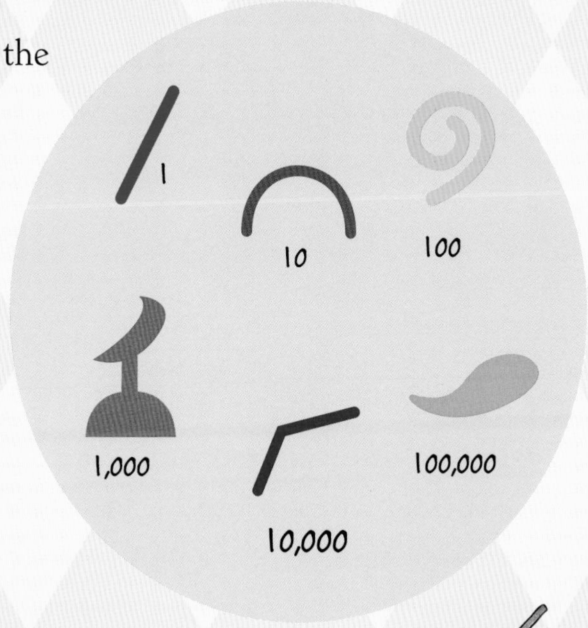

The finger stroke stood for 1.

The arch stood for 10.

The curved rope stood for 100.

The lotus flower stood for 1,000.

The bent finger stood for 10,000.

The tadpole stood for 100,000.

To show more than one of anything, the Egyptians repeated the symbol the correct number of times. The numeral below stood for 23:

∩∩///

But these numerals also meant 23:

/∩/∩/∩/   ∩//∩/∩/   ////∩∩

The Egyptians usually wrote their numerals from left to right. But sometimes they wrote them from right to left or from top to bottom.

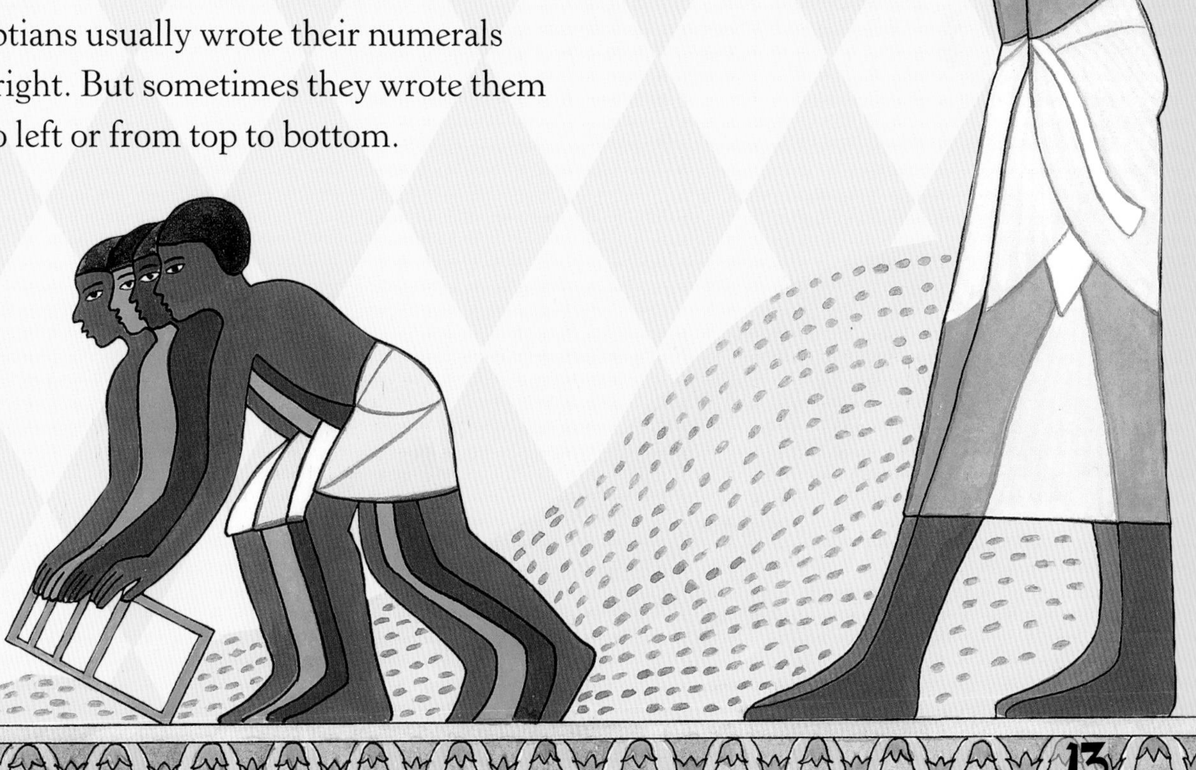

Numeral Systems

People all over the world invented different ways of writing numbers. Writing numbers a certain way is called a **numeral system.** By about 2100 B.C., the Babylonians used a system based on the number 60 instead of the number 10. The Babylonian numeral system is still with us today. It's why there are 60 seconds in a minute and 60 minutes in an hour.

Some ancient numeral systems were based on 60. We still use this system to count minutes and seconds.

The ancient Greeks and Romans used letters from their alphabet to stand for numbers. You have probably seen Roman **numerals** before. The letter I stands for 1. The letter V stands for 5, and X stands for 10.

The Roman numeral system uses letters. Today, Roman numerals are used to number the faces of clocks and to record dates on monuments and public buildings.

I	1
V	5
X	10
L	50
C	100
M	1000

TO HOBART TOWN LXIX MILES

The Maya made great advancements in mathematics and developed an accurate yearly calendar.

About 1,800 years ago, the Maya of Central America developed a numeral system based on the number 20. They must have used their fingers and their toes when counting. The Maya numerals for 1 to 10 looked like this:

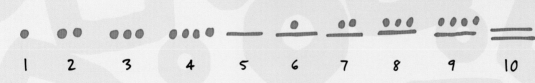

| 1 | 2 | 3 | 4 | 5 | 6 | 7 | 8 | 9 | 10 |

About 2,000 years ago, the Hindu people of India were using numerals that looked like this:

| 1 | 2 | 3 | 4 | 5 | 6 | 7 | 8 | 9 | 10 |

These Hindu numerals are very important to us. Over many years, and with some changes, they became the numerals we use today.

COUNTING WITH ANCIENT NUMERALS

You can practice counting with ancient **numerals**. Check your answers at the bottom of page 17.

Ancient Egypt was a country through which the Nile River flowed.

Count Like an Ancient Egyptian

Practice writing the Egyptian symbols shown on page 13. Then see if you can write these numerals in Egyptian:

1. 35

2. 112

3. 1,245

4. 10,437

5. 162,354

Count Like an Ancient Roman

Write the missing numerals for these problems.

1. Counting from 1 to 10:
   I, _____, III, IV, V, VI, _____, VIII, IX, _____

2. Counting by 10's to 150:
   _____, XX, XXX, XL, _____, LX, LXX, _____, XC, C, _____, CXX, CXXX, _____, CL

3. Now write these numbers in Roman numerals:
   a. 17
   b. 163
   c. 1,528

Ancient Rome was founded on the bank of the Tiber River in central Italy.

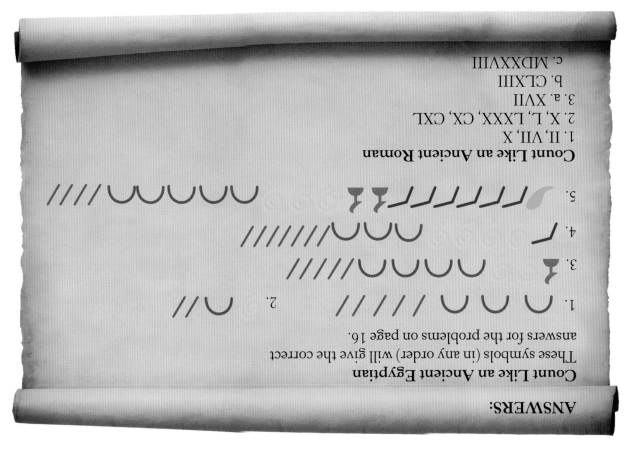

What Are Hindu and Arabic Numerals?

1

≡ ≥ **2**

≡ ≥ **3**

Do you remember the Hindu **numerals** invented 2,000 years ago that you learned about on page 15? When the Arabs conquered Spain about 1,300 years ago, they brought the Hindu numerals with them. Because the Arabs brought them, they became known as **Arabic numerals.**

Al-Khwarizmi was an Arab mathematician. He wrote a book that introduced a number system that spread from India and the Middle East to Europe.

The Hindu numeral 1 probably stands for one finger. The numeral 2 may have started as two straight lines that were later connected. Can you see the three straight lines in the numeral three?

AL=JUARISMI

Al-Gabr

Al-Muqabala

When the Arabs conquered Spain, the people of Europe were using Roman numerals. For several hundred years, they went right on using them. Most Europeans did their arithmetic with an **abacus.** When you use an abacus, it doesn't matter what your written number system is.

But over time, European mathematicians found that it was easier to write math problems with Arabic numerals than with Roman numerals. That's because Arabic numerals have a very important symbol: zero.

Today we use a number system that is based on Arabic numerals.

The Invention of Zero

The number zero probably doesn't seem all that special. But for most of history, people had no way to write zero. The Egyptian, Babylonian, and Roman **numeral systems** had no symbol for zero.

The Hindus and the Maya both invented zero. The English word *zero* comes from the Arabic *sifr,* which in turn came from the Hindu word *sunya*, meaning "empty."

Without zero, you can't write out numbers with **place value.** To understand place value, look at the **Arabic numeral** 203. The numeral has three "places": ones, tens, and hundreds. The numeral means "two hundreds, zero tens, and three ones."

𓂓𓏢 **CV** 105

Egyptian　　　　**Roman**　　　　**Arabic**

The ancient Romans did not use place value because they had no way of saying "no tens." The Romans would have written the Arabic numeral 105 as "CV." Such numerals are harder to work with than numerals with place value.

The invention of zero helped bankers keep track of their accounts. Banking developed in Italy during the 1200's.

What Is Addition?

Addition is a way of putting together two or more like things to find out how many there are all together.

Kelly and Nicky are collecting shells on a beach. Kelly has five shells. Nicky has three shells. How many shells do they have in all?

To find out, we use addition (uh DIHSH uhn). Addition means putting numbers or groups of things together.

+

=

One way to add is by "counting on." You know that Kelly has five shells. So you think, "five." Then you point to each of Nicky's shells and "count on" from five: "six, seven, eight." Together, Kelly and Nicky have eight shells.

You can write an addition statement like this:

$$5 + 3 = 8 \quad \text{or} \quad \begin{array}{r} 5 \\ + 3 \\ \hline 8 \end{array}$$

We say, "Five plus three equals eight."

Basic statements in addition are called addition facts. When you learn the addition facts, you will be able to add small groups of things quickly, without "counting on."

Here are some addition facts:

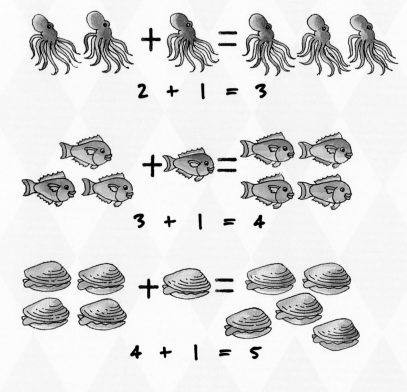

2 + 1 = 3

3 + 1 = 4

4 + 1 = 5

Do you see a pattern? Try following the pattern to complete these addition facts. (Answers appear on page 25.)

5 + 1 = _____

6 + 1 = _____

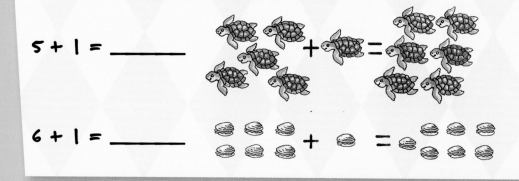

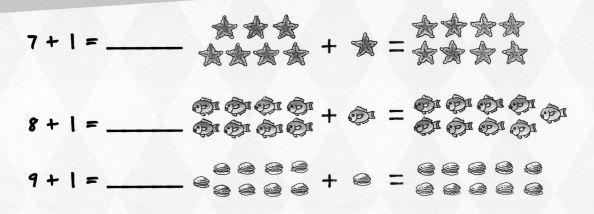

7 + 1 = _____

8 + 1 = _____

9 + 1 = _____

When you add 1 to any number, you get the next higher number.

Now look at these addition facts:

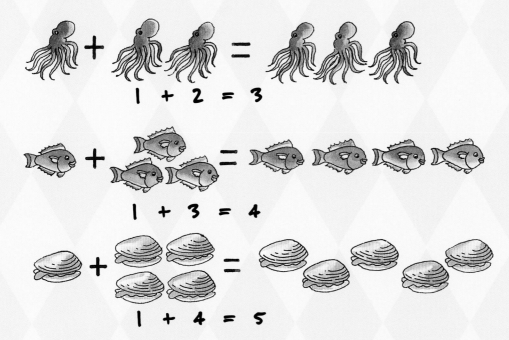

1 + 2 = 3

1 + 3 = 4

1 + 4 = 5

They are very similar to the first set of facts, aren't they? The first two numbers in each fact are switched. That's the only difference. The answer stays the same!

When you add numbers or groups of objects, you can put them in any order. You will always get the same answer.

Addition Facts

There are 100 basic addition facts. That's a lot, isn't it? But you can learn them all easily if you look for patterns in addition.

A table of basic addition facts appears on page 27. To find the answer to a problem like 1 + 3, look across the row that starts with 1 and down the column that starts with 3. Where the row and column meet, you will find the answer.

Have fun looking for patterns in the table! Here are some questions to get you started. (Answers appear at the bottom of the page.)

1. What happens when you add 0 to a number?

2. Where can you find the answers to problems like 1 + 1, 2 + 2, 3 + 3, and so on?

+	0	1	2	3	4	5	6	7	8	9
0	0	1	2	3	4	5	6	7	8	9
1	1	2	3	4	5	6	7	8	9	10
2	2	3	4	5	6	7	8	9	10	11
3	3	4	5	6	7	8	9	10	11	12
4	4	5	6	7	8	9	10	11	12	13
5	5	6	7	8	9	10	11	12	13	14
6	6	7	8	9	10	11	12	13	14	15
7	7	8	9	10	11	12	13	14	15	16
8	8	9	10	11	12	13	14	15	16	17
9	9	10	11	12	13	14	15	16	17	18

ANSWERS:

1. When you add 0 to any number, you get the same number.

2. The answers to problems like 1 + 1, 2 + 2, 3 + 3 (and so on) form a diagonal line from the top left to the bottom right of the chart.

YOU CAN ADD

Now try some addition problems on your own. Read each problem. Put counters in the small bowls to show the numbers you need to add. Then move all the counters into the third bowl. How many are there? (Answers appear on page 29.)

Problem #1

Kyoko has 4 computer games. Her aunt gives her 1 computer game for her birthday. How many computer games does Kyoko have now?

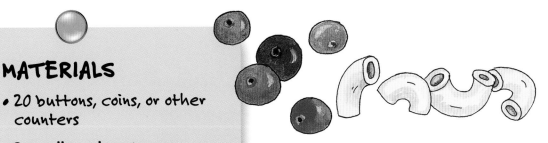

MATERIALS

- 20 buttons, coins, or other counters
- 2 small bowls or boxes
- Bigger bowl or box

Problem #2

Raul is at the library. He wants to check out 6 books about whales and 3 books about the planets. How many books does he want to check out?

Problem #3

There are 7 children playing baseball in the park. Then 5 more children join the game. How many children are playing baseball in all?

Problem #4

There are 11 girls and 9 boys in Yolanda's class. How many children are in the class?

What Is Subtraction?

Tanisha sees eight birds in a field. Two of them fly away. How many birds are left in the field?

Six birds are left in the field. Do you see them in the photograph on page 31?

Subtraction (suhb TRAK shuhn) means finding the difference between two numbers or two groups of things. Subtraction is the opposite of addition.

Look at the birds again. The difference between eight birds (in a field) and two birds (that flew away) is six birds. You can write this as a subtraction problem:

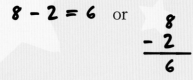

8 – 2 = 6   or

$$\begin{array}{r} 8 \\ -\ 2 \\ \hline 6 \end{array}$$

We say, "Eight minus two equals six."

Basic statements in subtraction are called subtraction facts. Here are some subtraction facts:

$$3 - 1 = 2 \qquad 4 - 1 = 3 \qquad 5 - 1 = 4$$

Do you see a pattern? Compare the subtraction facts with these addition facts:

$$2 + 1 = 3 \qquad 3 + 1 = 4 \qquad 4 + 1 = 5$$

Each basic subtraction fact is related to an addition fact:

$$2 + 1 = 3 \qquad\qquad 3 - 1 = 2$$

YOU CAN SUBTRACT

Now try some subtraction problems on your own. Read each problem. Put counters in the big bowl to show how many items you start with. Then move the correct number of counters into the small bowl. How many are left in the big bowl? (Answers appear on page 33.)

MATERIALS

- 20 buttons, coins, or other counters
- Small bowl or box
- Big bowl or box

Problem #1

Kyoko has 5 computer games. She gives 2 of them to her younger brother. How many computer games does Kyoko have now?

Problem #2

Raul has 9 library books at home. He has read 3 of them. How many books are left to read?

Problem #3

There were 12 children playing baseball in the park. Now 4 have to go home for supper. How many children are still playing baseball?

Problem #4

There are 20 children in Yolanda's class. Today, 1 is absent. How many children are in the classroom?

BACKWARD PUZZLES

Most number puzzles ask questions, and you find the answers. Here is a different kind of number puzzle. You are given the answers, and then you figure out how to get them!

Are you ready? Try this one:

The rules are simple:

• Use each number only once.

• You may add and subtract to get the answer.

PUZZLE I

The answer is 6.

Use any three numbers from 1 to 5.

Here is one solution:

$3 + 5 - 2 = 6$

(First add $3 + 5$ to get 8.

Then subtract 2 to get 6.)

What other solutions can you find?

Now try these puzzles.

How many ways can you solve each one?

PUZZLE 2

The answer is 8.

Use any three numbers from 1 to 10.

PUZZLE 3

The answer is 3.

Use any three numbers from 1 to 7.

35

What Is Multiplication?

Imagine that you are playing a game with dice. You roll five 4's:

You could add the 4's to find out how many points you have:

$$4 + 4 + 4 + 4 + 4 = 20$$

But once you learn that five 4's make 20, you know how to multiply! You can write the problem like this:

$$5 \times 4 = 20$$

We say, "Five times four equals twenty," or "Five fours are twenty."

Basic statements in **multiplication** are called multiplication facts. They're easy to learn if you know how to add.

Here are two more multiplication facts:

Six 2's are 12, and two 6's are 12. Try the **addition** yourself:

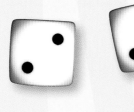

2 × 6 = 12

6 × 2 = 12

When you multiply two numbers, it doesn't matter which one you write first. Look at the eggs in the carton shown on this page. We can think of them as six rows of 2 or as two rows of 6. No matter which way you arrange the numbers, there are 12 eggs!

Counting Squares

For thousands of years, people didn't know about **multiplication.** When they wanted to know how many bricks were needed for a wall or how many tiles would cover a floor, they had to draw rows of squares. Then they counted the squares. Sometimes the counting took hours!

Multiplication is a fast way of counting numbers. It makes such tasks as counting the number of tiles needed to cover a floor easier.

A multiplication table is a chart that shows multiplication facts. To find the answer to a problem like 9 × 10, you look across the row that starts with 9 and down the row that starts with 10. Where the rows meet, you will find the answer!

Try this!

MultiPlication table

1	2	3	4	5	6	7	8	9	10
2	4	6	8	10	12	14	16	18	20
3	6	9	12	15	18	21	24	27	30
4	8	12	16	20	24	28	32	36	40
5	10	15	20	25	30	35	40	45	50
6	12	18	24	30	36	42	48	54	60
7	14	21	28	35	42	49	56	63	70
8	16	24	32	40	48	56	64	72	80
9	18	27	36	45	54	63	72	81	90
10	20	30	40	50	60	70	80	90	100

Today most people memorize multiplication facts instead of using a table. But you can check your answers with a multiplication table. Try a few problems and see!

1. 3 x 7 = ?

2. 8 x 5 = ?

3. 4 x 6 = ?

ANSWERS:
1. 21; 2. 40; 3. 24

Multiplication Tricks

Here are some tricks that will help you learn to multiply quickly:

Any number multiplied by 0 equals 0.

$$2 \times 0 = 0 \qquad 0 \times 2 = 0$$
$$9 \times 0 = 0 \qquad 0 \times 9 = 0$$

Any number multiplied by 1 equals itself.

$$2 \times 1 = 2 \qquad 1 \times 2 = 2$$
$$9 \times 1 = 9 \qquad 1 \times 9 = 9$$

To multiply a number by 10, just put a 0 to the right of your original number.

$$2 \times 10 = 20 \qquad 10 \times 2 = 20$$
$$9 \times 10 = 90 \qquad 10 \times 9 = 90$$

Multiplying by 9's is especially fun! You can do it on your fingers:

Choose a **multiplication** problem, such as 3 × 9. Hold up both hands, palms toward you. Then count three (for three 9's), starting from your left thumb. Fold down the third finger on your left hand. You will see two fingers before the one you folded down and seven fingers after it. That's the answer to your problem.

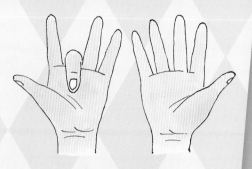

3 × 9 = 27

Now use your fingers to multiply 7 × 9. Count seven from your left thumb. Fold down your seventh finger, and there's the answer:

7 × 9 = 63

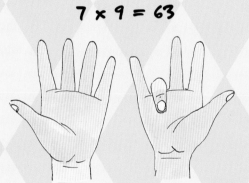

Try this!

Here's a multiplication trick that will amaze your friends: Ask a friend to pick a number and not tell you what it is. Get your friend to multiply the number by 2 and then by 5. Then ask for the answer.

When you hear the answer, you will know what number he or she picked! Here's how the trick works: The answer your friend says will end in a 0. Simply drop the 0 and you will know what number your friend picked. For example, suppose your friend picks the number 4. 4 × 2 = 8, and 8 × 5 equals 40. When you hear the answer 40, drop the 0 and you'll know your friend picked the number 4!

What Is Division?

Imagine you are playing outside with three friends on a hot summer day. Your mother brings out a box of 12 popsicles. She says you may eat them all, but you must divide them evenly. How many popsicles will each of you get?

To solve this problem, you could keep subtracting four popsicles (one for each child) from 12 popsicles until nothing is left:

$$12 - 4 = 8 \qquad 8 - 4 = 4 \qquad 4 - 4 = 0$$

You can subtract four from 12 three times. This means that there are three 4's in 12. Each of you will get three popsicles!

Once you learn that, you know how to divide. **Division** is a way of separating a group of things into equal parts.

You can write the problem like this:

$$12 \div 4 = 3$$

We say, "Twelve divided by four equals three."

Basic statements in division are called division facts. Here are two more division facts:

$$12 \div 6 = 2$$

$$12 \div 2 = 6$$

Do they look familiar? Compare them to these **multiplication** facts:

$$6 \times 2 = 12$$

$$2 \times 6 = 12$$

If you can multiply, you won't have trouble dividing because division is the opposite of multiplication!

What Are Fractions?

Fractions come from breaking something into equal parts.

Sometimes numbers don't divide evenly. For example, what is 8 divided by 3? No whole number gives the answer. The answer is somewhere in between 2 and 3—it's 2 and 2/3.

2/3 is a **fraction.** Fractions come from breaking something into equal parts. Fractions are written as two numbers separated by a line:

2/5

The fraction 2/5 stands for two parts of something that has been broken into five equal parts.

Try this!

If you've ever baked, you've used fractions. Look in your kitchen for measuring cups. Can you measure out 2/3 cups of flour? How about 3/4 cups of flour? What fraction has a greater amount of flour: 2/3 or 3/4?

Some fractions have special names. When something is broken into two equal parts, each part is called a half. When it is broken into three equal parts, each part is called a third. And when it is broken into four equal parts, each part is called a fourth, or a quarter. The names for most other parts are made by adding *-th* to the end of the word that shows the number of equal parts. So the word for 2/5 is two-fifths. The word for 3/10 is three-tenths.

Fractions allow people to express amounts that are less than a whole.

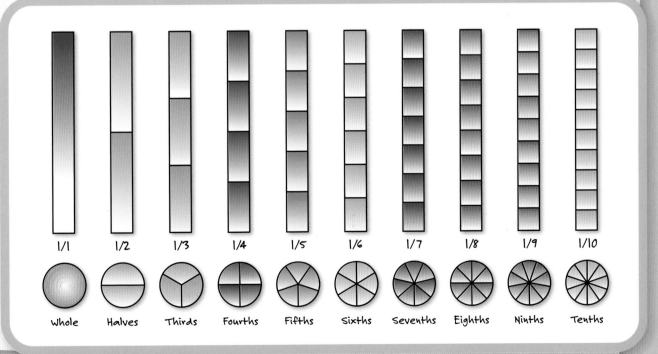

45

Heads or Tails

Coin tosses are used in sports to determine which team gets control of the ball first.

Rick wanted to go to the video arcade. Gayle wanted to go swimming. They agreed to toss a coin to decide what they would do.

"Heads or tails?" asked Rick as he flipped the coin.

"Tails never fails!" called Gayle. Sure enough, the coin landed with the tails side up.

"See?" Gayle grinned. "I told you that tails never fails! Swimming it is."

Do you think Gayle is right? Does tails win more often than heads? Try this experiment and find out.

Try this!

Tally marks are an easy way to keep track of numbers when you're counting. Use four straight lines to represent the first four things. Then draw another line through the four lines to represent the fifth thing. Start with another line for the sixth thing. When you're finished marking, count the groups of five and add the few remaining lines as ones.

HHT = 5

HHT HHT = 10

HHT II = 7

Make two columns on a piece of paper. Label them "Heads" and "Tails." Flip a coin 50 times. On your paper, mark which side shows after each flip. Use tally marks.

Count the marks in each column. There may be a few more heads or a few more tails, but the numbers should be almost the same.

Every time you flip a coin, the chance that it will come up heads is exactly the same as the chance that it will come up tails. We say that the chances are even.

HEADS

HHT II

TAILS

HHT I

What Are the Chances?

When you flip a coin, the chances of getting heads are the same as the chances of getting tails. Rolling a die is similar, but a die has six sides. The chances of rolling a 1 are the same as the chances of rolling a 2, 3, 4, 5, or 6.

Everything changes when you roll two or more dice. Imagine that you and a friend are playing a game with two dice. Pretend that if you roll a 12, you'll win the game, but if your friend rolls a 7, she'll win.

Which of you is more likely to win? Or are your chances about the same?

Try this!

Roll a pair of dice 50 times. Keep track of the numbers that come up. Which numbers come up most often?

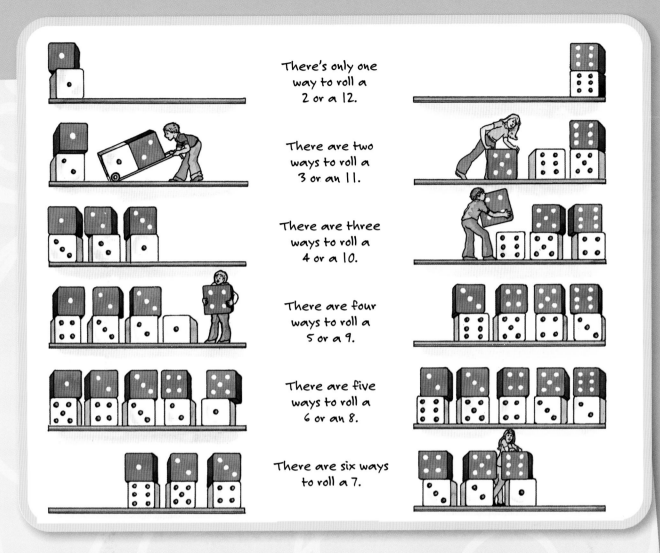

There's only one way to roll a 2 or a 12.

There are two ways to roll a 3 or an 11.

There are three ways to roll a 4 or a 10.

There are four ways to roll a 5 or a 9.

There are five ways to roll a 6 or an 8.

There are six ways to roll a 7.

When you roll two dice and add their numbers, you get a number between 2 and 12. There are 36 possible combinations of two dice.

There is only one way to get a 12. You have to roll two 6's. So you have one chance out of 36 (1/36) to roll a 12.

But there are six ways to get a 7. So your friend has six chances out of 36 (6/36) to roll a 7. That means her chance of winning the game is better than yours!

This illustration shows the number of ways you can roll different number combinations with dice.

STATISTICS AND SPORTS

Statistics are numbers that give us information. For example, they may tell us how many people live in a city—and how many of them own cars or televisions. They may tell the average (usual) temperature of your city on any date.

Statistics are an important part of sports, too! They tell how many games your favorite team has won and lost. They tell which soccer player has made the most goals this season. They tell which basketball player scores the most points per game.

Joel, Ahmed, and Fernando play on a soccer team called the Rockets. The Rockets played four games this month. See how many goals Joel, Ahmed, and Fernando got in each game:

Game	1	2	3	4
Joel	4	1	2	0
Ahmed	1	0	1	2
Fernando	2	3	1	2

Use the chart above to answer these questions:

1. Which player made the most goals in one game?

2. Which player made the most total goals?

Player	Points Scored
Carmen	10
Josie	3
Alexis	7
Maya	2
Nujanart	0
Debby	4
Kirsten	8
Tanika	4
Patricia	0
Chris	0
Elena	2
Jean	0

Some statistics for players of a basketball team called the Stars appear on this page. See how many points each player scored in the last game.

Use the chart on this page to answer these questions:

3. How many points did the team score?

4. Which player scored the most points?

5. How many players are on the team?

ANSWERS:
1. Joel made the most goals in one game (4 goals in Game 1);
2. Fernando made the most total goals (8);
3. The basketball team scored 40 points;
4. Carmen scored the most points (10);
5. There are 12 players on the team

Getting Graphic

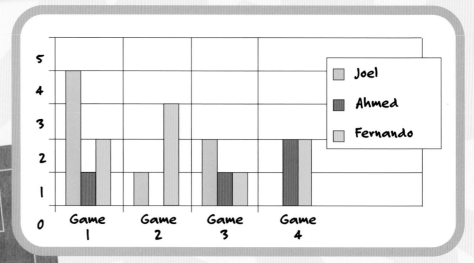

A **graph** (GRAF) is a picture. Graphs show **statistics** in a way that is easy to understand. There are many kinds of graphs.

The graph above is a bar graph. It shows how many goals Joel, Ahmed, and Fernando made in four soccer games.

The numbers on the left are the number of goals. Joel's goals are shown in blue, Ahmed's goals are in red, and Fernando's goals are in yellow. Notice that Ahmed made 0 goals in Game 2.

1. Who made 0 goals in Game 4?

2. Who made the most goals in one game? You can tell very quickly by looking at the bar graph.

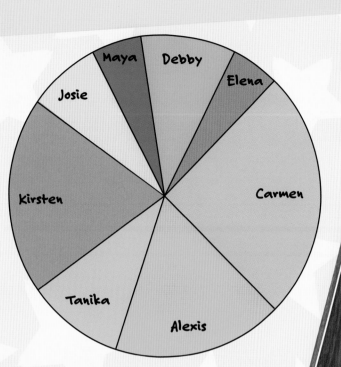

Above is a circle graph, or "pie chart." It shows the points scored by members of the Stars basketball team during a game.

The circle stands for the total number of points scored by the team (40). Each colored section stands for the points scored by a particular player. There are no sections for players who scored 0 points.

3. Which section is the biggest? What does that tell us?

Calculators and Computers

Calculators and computers are tools that can help you do work.

You would probably have no trouble multiplying 2 × 2 and 4 × 4 in your head. But what about 256 × 256? It would take a while to solve that problem, even with a pencil and paper!

Many people use computers and calculators to solve problems involving big numbers. These machines can solve difficult math problems in the blink of an eye—and they never make mistakes!

Most calculators are easy to use. To enter a problem, you press a series of keys. Tiny electronic circuits inside the calculator find the answer. Almost immediately, the answer appears on a display window.

Calculators add, subtract, multiply, and divide quickly and without making mistakes.

Computers often have calculator programs that work like pocket calculators. Simple calculators are useful for everyday tasks. Scientists and mathematicians use more complicated calculators and computer programs.

Computers are like giant calculators that process information at great speeds.

CALCULATOR GAMES

Calculators are great for solving problems. They are also fun to use! Try these games with a simple calculator. If you haven't used a calculator before, ask an adult for help (and permission).

Square Tricks

1. Think of a number. Enter it into the calculator.

2. Multiply the number by itself and write down the answer.

3. Press clear. Then enter your first number.

4. Add 1 and press the equals key.

5. Square that number (multiply the number by itself).

6. Subtract the number you have written down in step 2.

7. Subtract 1.

8. Subtract your first number.

The answer will be your original number!

Magic Nines

1. Write down a four-digit number (for example, 1,735). Don't use a number like 1,111 or 5,555 that has all four digits alike.

2. Mix up the digits to make a new number (for example, 7,513). Write down that number, too.

3. Which number is bigger? Enter it into your calculator.

4. Subtract the smaller number. Write down the answer.

5. Add up the digits in the answer. If you get a number with more than one digit, add those digits together.

No matter what number you start with, the answer will always be a multiple of 9!

What Are Binary Numbers?

You might be wondering how, exactly, calculators and computers do arithmetic. Humans can add and subtract by counting on our fingers, using an **abacus,** or writing down symbols on paper. Computers don't even have fingers. How do they work?

People today count with **Arabic numerals,** which use ten symbols: 0, 1, 2, 3, 4, 5, 6, 7, 8, and 9. We only use ten symbols because we have ten fingers.

Computers can also count. They use **binary numbers.** The binary system is sometimes called base 2. A binary number is written with only two symbols: 0 and 1. Instead of fingers, a computer has circuits. Each circuit can be switched on or off—on for 1, and off for 0.

Any Arabic number can also be written as a binary number. The numbers are the same. They are just written differently.

Computers use binary numbers as a kind of language.

Binary numbers are like a code that a computer uses to operate. Codes can also be used by people as a form of communication. Before the invention of the telephone, people used a device called a telegraph to send messages by using electric current. The sender tapped out electrical signals in Morse code, a system of dots and dashes. A person who knew Morse code listened to the clicks and wrote down each letter so that the message could be read.

A code can be a system of letters, numbers, or other symbols that stand for letters or words in a message. For example, you could make up a code where each number stands for a letter: 1 = A, 2 = B, 3 = C, and so on.

Here is a message in a different code. Again, each number stands for a letter. See if you can figure out the code and read the message. You'll need a piece of paper and a pencil to work through the code. (Hint: 2 = Y.)

8 22 24 9 22 7   14 22 8 8 26 20 22

Here are more secret messages! See if you can decode them—undo the code and read the messages. Some codes use **numerals,** and others use letters. Once you figure out how a code works, you can use it to send messages to your friends! If you get stuck, you can use the hints shown on this page. You can check your answers at the bottom of this page.

1. GSV ZOKSZYVG RH
   GFIMVW ZILFMW

2. ITI SALLIN HO WYO
   ULOO KATIT

3. 2 11 19 23 2 21 14 3   21 7
   20 25 14

4. HKZ XVWW RUUV
   IVMGO BZMWYZ XPDZIW

HINTS

1. Think backward!

2. Look at this message carefully!

3. 1 = A, 2 = D, 3 = G

4. This code combines two of the other codes. Decode the message once, then look at it carefully.

ANSWERS:
1. the alphabet is turned around
2. it is all in how you look at it
3. decoding is fun
4. spaced differently and backward

Glossary

abacus a counting tool that has beads that slide on wires inside a wooden frame.

Arabic numerals the most common symbols used to represent numbers. The basic symbols, called *digits,* are 0, 1, 2, 3, 4, 5, 6, 7, 8, and 9. The position of a digit in an Arabic numeral determines its value.

binary number a number written using only two digits (1 and 0). Computers use binary numbers as a kind of language.

division a way of breaking a number into smaller equal numbers. A division problem may look like this: 6 ÷ 2 = 3.

fraction one or more of the equal parts of a whole number.

graph a picture that shows relationships between numbers. Common kinds of graphs include bar graphs, line graphs, and pie charts.

multiplication a fast way of adding numbers that are the same. A multiplication problem may look like this: 4 × 2 = 8.

numerals written marks or symbols that stand for numbers.

numeral system a way of counting and naming numbers.

place value the value, or meaning, of a numeral that comes from its position in a string of numerals. In the numeral 527, the 5 stands for five 100's. It has a higher place value than the 7, which stands for seven 1's. Whether a number means 1's, 10's, or more depends on the place it appears in a string of numerals.

statistics numbers that give information. They often describe groups of people or objects. Statistics about your family might include the number of people, their ages, their heights, and how many of them like chocolate ice cream.

Find Out More

Books

Fabulous Fractions: Games and Activities That Make Math Easy and Fun by Lynette Long (Wiley, 2001)

Fun with Roman Numerals by David A. Adler and Edward Miller (Holiday House, 2008)

Math Detectives: Finding Fun in Numbers by Lalie Harcourt and others (Sterling Publishing, 2002)

Math Dictionary for Kids: The Essential Guide to Math Terms, Strategies, and Tables by Theresa Fitzgerald (Prufrock Press, 2006)

Pigs, Cows, and Probability by Marcie Aboff (Capstone Press, 2011)

The Story of Our Numbers: The History of Arabic Numbers by Zelda King (PowerKids Press, 2004)

Used Any Numbers Lately? by Susan Allen, Jane Lindaman, and Vicky Enright (Millbrook Press, 2008)

Websites

Biographies of Women Mathematicians
http://www.agnesscott.edu/lriddle/women/women.htm
This website focuses on the contributions of women in the field of mathematics.

Cool Math 4 Kids
http://www.coolmath.com/
Lessons, practice activities, and flashcards make this website a useful resource for kids interested in any kind of math skills.

Figure This! Math Challenges for Families
http://www.figurethis.org/index.html
At this site, fun challenges for the whole family bring out the many uses of math in everyday life.

Mathographies
http://scidiv.bellevuecollege.edu/Math/MathFolks.html
Learn about the people behind the numbers in this collection of biographies.

Math Playground
http://www.MathPlayground.com/
The Math Playground lets you test your math skills with word problems and logic puzzles. The site also features educational videos and flash cards.

Mathslice
http://www.mathslice.com/
Mathslice.com provides lessons and tips on many different math skills and concepts, along with a large selection of games to help you practice what you've learned.

NCES Kids Zone
http://nces.ed.gov/nceskids/chances/index.asp
Graphing, probability, and other concepts are explored in detail at this educational site from the U.S. Department of Education.

Index

Activities